Chimpanzees

ABDO
Publishing Company

A Buddy Book
by
Julie Murray

Published by Buddy Books, an imprint of ABDO Publishing Company, 4940 Viking Drive, Suite 622, Edina, Minnesota 55435. Copyright © 2002 by Abdo Consulting Group, Inc. International copyrights reserved in all countries. No part of this book may be reproduced in any form without written permission from the publisher.

Printed in the United States.

Edited by: Christy DeVillier
Contributing Editors: Matt Ray, Michael P. Goecke
Graphic Design: Maria Hosley
Image Research: Deborah Coldiron
Photographs: Eyewire, Minden Pictures

Library of Congress Cataloging-in-Publication Data

Murray, Julie, 1969-
   Chimpanzees/Julie Murray.
      p. cm. — (Animal kingdom)
   Summary: Introduces the habitat and characteristics of chimpanzees, and briefly describes Jane Goodall's work with them.
   ISBN 1-57765-713-6
      1. Chimpanzee—Juvenile literature. [1. Chimpanzee.] I. Title. II. Animal kingdom
   (Edina, Minn.)

QL737.P96 M873 2002
599.885—dc21

                                                     2001045891

Contents

Great Apes

What do chimpanzees, gorillas, orangutans, and bonobos have in common? All of these animals are great apes. Great apes are bigger than monkeys and lemurs. Great apes do not have tails. Chimpanzees are the smallest of the great apes. Chimpanzees may also be the smartest.

Chimpanzees are great apes.

Chimpanzees And People

Great apes are primates. Primates have large brains. They have eyes that look forward. People belong to the primate group, too.

Chimpanzees, or chimps, have a lot in common with people. Can you grab things with your hands? Can you communicate with your family and friends? Can you use tools? Chimps can do all of these things, too.

Do chimps have some of the same feelings as people?

Like people, chimps tickle each other. Chimps hug and kiss each other. Many people believe chimps feel joy, sadness, and fear.

Talking To Chimps

Some people teach chimps American Sign Language. American Sign Language is talking with your hands. Chimps can talk to people and other chimps through "signing."

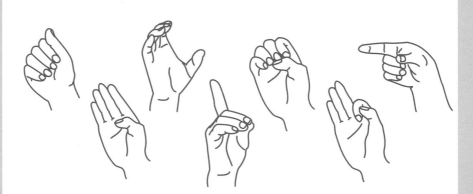

What They Look Like

Chimpanzees have dark fur all over. This hair does not grow on a chimp's face and ears. Parts of a chimp's hands and feet are hairless, too.

A chimp's fur can be black or brown.

Chimpanzees are about four feet (one meter) tall. A grown male chimp can weigh as much as 120 pounds (54 kg). Female chimps are smaller.

These **primates** are strong for their size. Chimps are three times stronger than people!

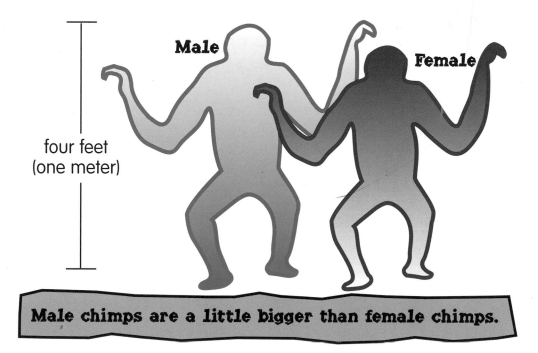

four feet (one meter)

Male

Female

Male chimps are a little bigger than female chimps.

The Chimpanzee's Home

Chimps spend a lot of time in trees.

Chimpanzees live in parts of central and western Africa. They like rain forests, grasslands, and woodlands.

Chimpanzees are **arboreal** animals. An arboreal animal spends most of its life in trees. Trees are a safe place for chimps. **Predators** cannot always catch chimps high in the trees.

A mother chimp rests with her baby in their treetop nest.

At night, chimps sleep in the trees. They build nests with branches and leaves. These nests are soft beds for the sleeping chimps.

Everyday Life

Chimpanzees **groom** each other often. They stroke each other's fur. They pick out insects, dirt, and seeds. Grooming keeps them clean. Chimps often groom each other after a fight. Grooming calms an excited chimp.

Chimps make and use stick tools to catch termites.

Finding food is a big part of a chimpanzee's day. Chimps eat leaves, flowers, seeds, fruits, insects, nuts, and meat. Chimps can use a stick as a tool to catch termites. They use rocks to crack open nuts. Chimpanzees hunt small animals for meat, too.

Chimp Communities

Chimpanzees live in groups, or **communities**. These communities can have as many as 120 chimps. A male chimp stays in one community his whole life. Some female chimps join new communities when they become adults.

Young chimps learn from the older chimps in their community.

Each chimp has a place, or rank, in its community. The community's leader is always a male chimp. This chimp leader is the alpha male. The alpha male is the toughest chimp. He wins his role by scaring the other chimps.

Baby Chimps

It takes years for a chimpanzee to grow up. Young chimps stay close to their mothers for many years. A baby chimp sleeps in its mother's nest. It drinks its mother's milk until age five or older.

Most chimps are adults by the age of 15. Chimpanzees can live for more than 50 years.

Young chimps stay close to their mothers.

Jane Goodall

Jane Goodall spent almost 30 years studying chimpanzees in Tanzania, Africa. She was the first to discover that chimps used tools and hunted. Jane's studies show that chimps are like us in many ways. Her discovery has changed everyone's ideas about primates.

Today, Jane works hard giving speeches and writing letters. She hopes to make the world a better place for all living things.

"Let us develop respect for all living things."
-Jane Goodall

Important Words

alpha male a chimpanzee community's leader.

arboreal animals that spend most of their lives in trees.

communicate giving and receiving information. Talking and writing are two ways to communicate.

community a group of chimpanzees living together.

groom to clean and care for.

predator an animal that hunts other animals (prey) for food.

primate a group that people, great apes, and monkeys belong to.

Web Sites

All about Chimpanzees

www.enchantedlearning.com/subjects/apes/chimp/
In addition to many facts about chimps, this web site offers a quiz and a chimp picture to print out and color.

African Primates at Home

www.indiana.edu/%7Eprimate/primates.html
See and hear chimps at this web site.

Animal Bytes: Chimpanzee

www.seaworld.org/AnimalBytes/chimpanzeeab.html
There are plenty of fun facts about chimps here.

Index